W9-BEC-783

## DATE DUE

|  |  |  |  |
|---|---|---|---|
|  |  |  |  |
|  |  |  |  |
|  |  |  |  |
|  |  |  |  |
|  |  |  |  |
|  |  |  |  |
|  |  |  |  |
|  |  |  |  |
|  |  |  |  |
|  |  |  |  |
|  |  |  |  |
|  |  |  |  |
|  |  |  |  |
|  |  |  |  |

# MOUNTAINS

## My World of Geography

## Angela Royston
Heinemann Library
Chicago, Illinois

© 2005 Heinemann Library
a division of Reed Elsevier Inc.
Chicago, Illinois

Customer Service  888-454-2279
Visit our website at www.heinemannlibrary.com

Design: Ron Kamen and Celia Jones
Illustrations: Barry Atkinson Barry Atkinson (pp. 8, 17), Jo Brooker (p. 15), Jeff Edwards (pp. 5, 28–29)
Photo Research: Rebecca Sodergren, Melissa Allison, and Debra Weatherley
Originated by Ambassador Litho
Printed and bound in Hong Kong and China by South China Printing

09 08 07 06 05
10 9 8 7 6 5 4 3 2 1

**Library of Congress
Cataloging-in-Publication Data**

Royston, Angela.
  Mountains / Angela Royston.
    p. cm. – (My world of geography)
  Includes bibliographical references and index.
  ISBN 1-4034-5592-9
  1. Mountains–Juvenile literature. I. Title. II. Series.
  GB512.R69 2005
  551.43'2–dc22

                              2004003868

**Acknowledgments**

The author and publisher are grateful to the following for permission to reproduce copyright material:
pp. 4, 18 (Robert Essel NYC), 19 (Ray Juno), 24 Corbis; p. 6 NASA; pp. 7 (Digital Vision), 25 (Photodisc) Getty Images; pp. 9 (Simon Fraser), 13 (Bernhard Edmaier) Science Photo Library; pp. 10 (Douglas Peebles), 20 (Imagestate/S. Barnett), 21 (Phototake Inc./Peter Treiber), 26 (Gallen Rowell) Alamy Images; p. 11 (Tudor Photography) Harcourt Education Ltd.; p. 12 Nature Picture Library; pp. 14, 16 John Cleare Mountain Picture Library; p. 22 Robert Harding Picture Library; p. 27 Bruce Coleman.

Map on page 23 reproduced by permission of Ordnance Survey on behalf of the Controller of Her Majesty's Stationary Office, © Crown Copyright 100000230.

Cover photograph reproduced with permission of Getty Images/Stone.

Every effort has been made to contact copyright holders of any material reproduced in this book. Any omissions will be rectified in subsequent printings if notice is given to the publisher.

# Contents

Some words are shown in bold, **like this.** You can find out what they mean by looking in the glossary.

# What Is a Mountain?

A mountain is a rocky piece of land that is much higher than the land around it. The top of a mountain is called the **summit.**

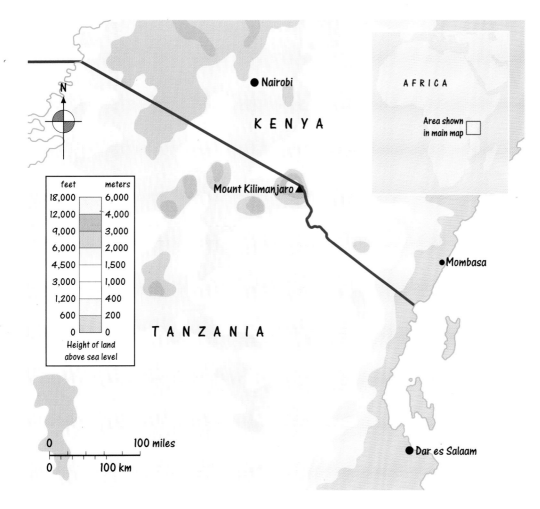

● Nairobi

K E N Y A

A F R I C A

Area shown
in main map

Mount Kilimanjaro ▲

●Mombasa

| feet | meters |
|---|---|
| 18,000 | 6,000 |
| 12,000 | 4,000 |
| 9,000 | 3,000 |
| 6,000 | 2,000 |
| 4,500 | 1,500 |
| 3,000 | 1,000 |
| 1,200 | 400 |
| 600 | 200 |
| 0 | 0 |

Height of land
above sea level

T A N Z A N I A

0          100 miles

0      100 km

● Dar es Salaam

This map shows Mount Kilimanjaro in
Africa. The mountain is shown by a
black triangle. The height of the land
is shown in different colors. The
highest land is colored light purple.

# Mountain Ranges

Most mountains are part of a mountain **range.** A range is a long chain of mountains that lie close together. Some mountain ranges stretch for thousands of miles.

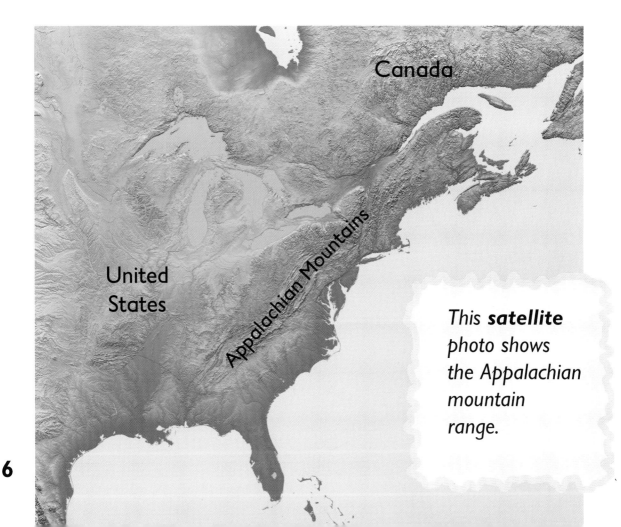

Canada

United States

Appalachian Mountains

*This **satellite** photo shows the Appalachian mountain range.*

mountain

foothill

The mountains in the middle of a range are usually the highest. The hills around the edge are lower. They are called **foothills.**

# Measuring Mountains

In this diagram, mountains 1, 2, and 3 are all the same height. This is because mountains are always measured from their top down to sea level.

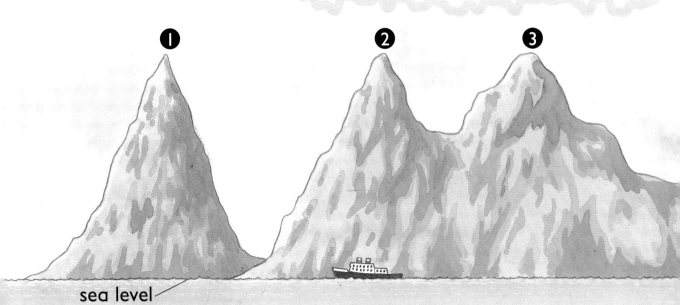

sea level

The height of a mountain is measured from its top to **sea level.** This way of measuring mountains is used all over the world.

People use many special **instruments** to measure the height of mountains. Sometimes the instruments are carried on an airplane or a **satellite.**

*This climber is measuring the height of a mountain.*

# How Mountains Form

Most mountains form very slowly over millions of years. Huge forces from deep inside Earth move parts of the land. Some of the land rises slowly.

These mountains are in Alaska. They are getting a bit higher every year.

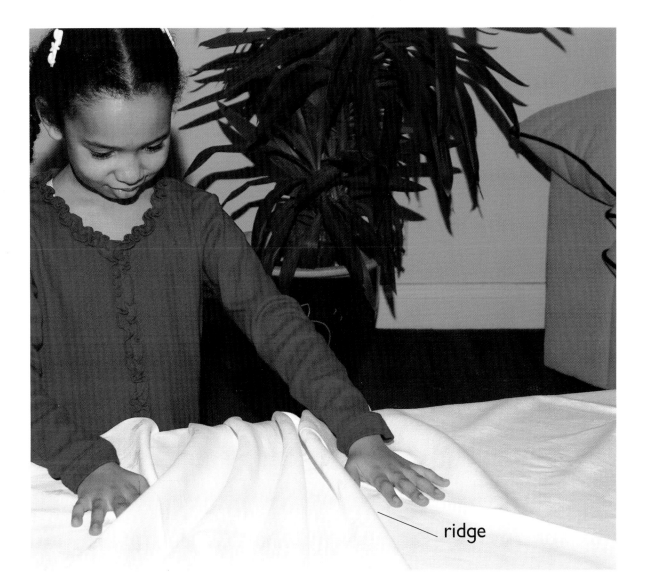

ridge

You can see the way some mountains are made by pushing a tablecloth on a smooth table. The cloth forms a ridge when it is pushed.

# Volcanoes

Many mountains are made by **volcanoes.** When a volcano **erupts,** hot, melted rock called **lava** spills out from deep inside Earth. The new rock cools and becomes hard.

lava

volcano

Each time a volcano erupts, new rock piles up higher and higher. Some volcanoes are still erupting. Other volcanoes stopped erupting long ago.

*This volcano is on the island of Lanzarote in Spain. It stopped erupting many years ago.*

# Wearing Down Rocks

Mountains are changing all the time. The weather slowly wears them down. Wind, sunshine, rain, and snow break up the rocks that form the mountain.

mountaintop

rocky slope

*Sometimes a whole cliff breaks up and falls down the mountainside!*

14

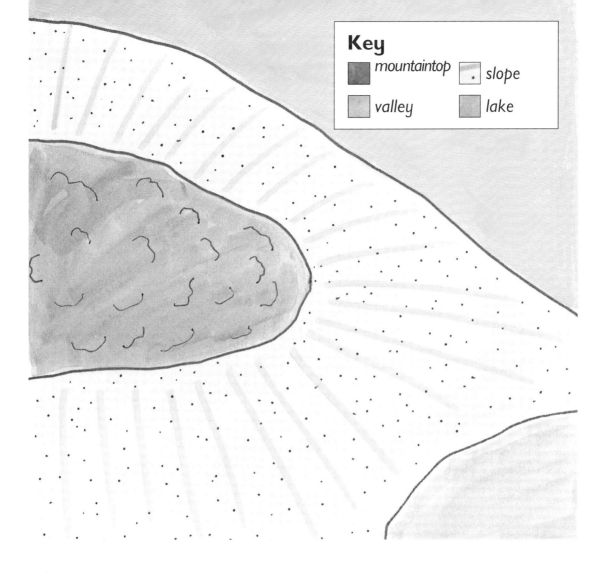

This map shows the same mountain as the photo on page 14. Some of the **cliff** has fallen down to form a rocky slope. You could draw a map like this.

# Mountain Weather

The weather becomes colder as you go higher up a mountain. The tops of the highest mountains are so cold that snow always covers them.

This **mountaineer** is dressed in very warm clothes because the weather is so cold.

a lot of rain

mountains

dry land or desert

The type of weather on one side of a mountain **range** is often different from the other side. One side of the range may be very wet, but on the other side, there may be a **desert.**

17

# Farming

People use the warm lower slopes of a mountain to farm. Farmers shape the sides of the mountain into flat areas called **terraces.** It is easier to grow **crops** on flat areas of land.

*Terraces are like huge steps cut into the sides of a mountain.*

The higher slopes on a mountain are often grassy. In summer, farmers take **cattle,** sheep, and goats up to the higher slopes to feed on the grass.

# Mining

Some rocks contain valuable **metals.** Rocks in the Andes Mountains in South America contain copper, tin, gold, and silver.

*This rock has gold in it.*

People dig rocks out of **mines.** They separate metal from the rocks. Then they carry the rocks and metal down the mountainside in trucks.

*This man is working in a gold mine.*

# Finding Your Way

It is fun to walk or climb in the mountains. Sometimes you can follow a path. A map and a **compass** can help you find your way.

This map shows an area of Wales in the United Kingdom. It might be used by walkers, so they don't get lost.

On this map the dotted lines are paths. The yellow lines are roads. The blue lines are streams and rivers. The brown loopy lines are **contour** lines. Contour lines show how steep and high up the places on the map are.

23

# Enjoying Mountains

Mountains are wild and beautiful places. Many people like to climb to the top of mountains and enjoy the views.

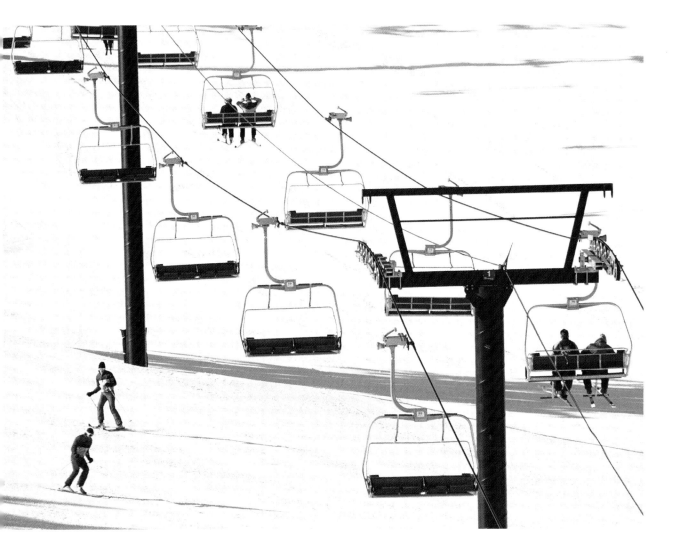

Some people use mountain slopes for snow skiing. **Ski lifts** carry them to the tops of the slopes. Then they push themselves off the lifts and ski down the slopes.

# Protecting Mountains

All mountains wear down slowly over time, but some mountains are being worn down too quickly. So many people climb the mountains that the paths become damaged.

*This bear is catching a salmon in a national park in Alaska.*

Many mountains are turned into **national parks.** This means that the animals that live there are protected. People also cannot dig **mines** in national parks.

# Mountains of the World

**Mount McKinley**
Key fact: Mount McKinley is the highest
mountain in North America.
Height: 20,320 feet
(6,194 meters)

▲ Mount McKinley

NORTH
AMERICA

Rockies

Appalachian
Mountains

▲ Mount Kea

**Mount Aconcagua**
Key fact: Mount Aconcagua is the highest
mountain in South America.
Height: 22,834 feet
(6,960 meters)

SOUTH
AMERICA

Andes

▲ Mount Aconcagua

This map shows the biggest
mountain **ranges** and some of the
highest mountains in the world.

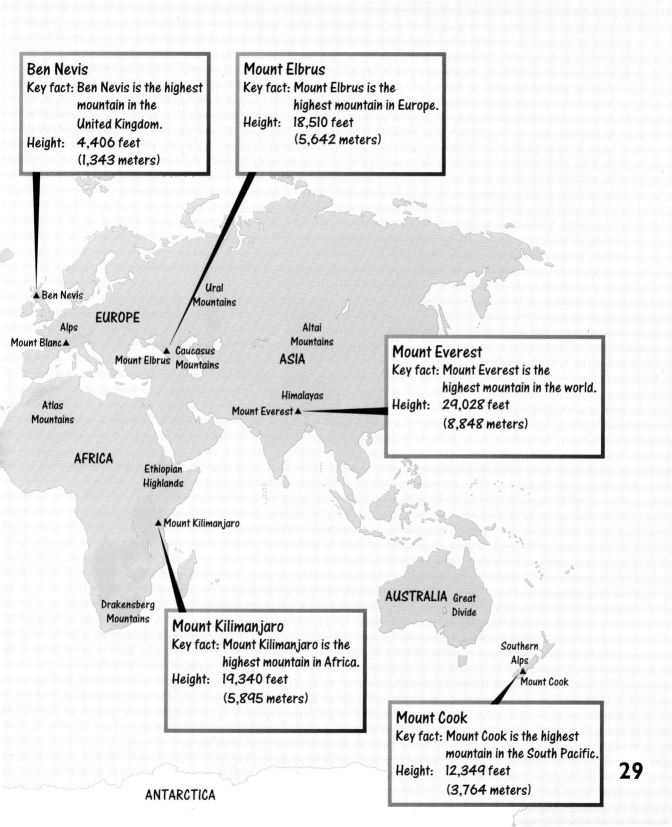

**Ben Nevis**
Key fact: Ben Nevis is the highest
            mountain in the
            United Kingdom.
Height:    4,406 feet
            (1,343 meters)

**Mount Elbrus**
Key fact: Mount Elbrus is the
            highest mountain in Europe.
Height:    18,510 feet
            (5,642 meters)

▲ Ben Nevis

**EUROPE**

Ural
Mountains

Alps

Mount Blanc▲

▲ Mount Elbrus

Caucasus
Mountains

Altai
Mountains

**ASIA**

**Mount Everest**
Key fact: Mount Everest is the
            highest mountain in the world.
Height:    29,028 feet
            (8,848 meters)

Atlas
Mountains

Himalayas

Mount Everest▲

**AFRICA**

Ethiopian
Highlands

▲ Mount Kilimanjaro

Drakensberg
Mountains

**AUSTRALIA** Great
            Divide

**Mount Kilimanjaro**
Key fact: Mount Kilimanjaro is the
            highest mountain in Africa.
Height:    19,340 feet
            (5,895 meters)

Southern
Alps

▲ Mount Cook

**Mount Cook**
Key fact: Mount Cook is the highest
            mountain in the South Pacific.
Height:    12,349 feet
            (3,764 meters)

**29**

ANTARCTICA

# Glossary

**cattle** cows, bulls, or oxen

**cliff** very steep slope

**compass** instrument that shows the directions (north, south, east, west)

**contour** line on a map that shows how high a place is

**crop** plant grown for food

**desert** area of very dry land, where there is not much rain

**erupt** burst out

**foothill** hill on the edge of a mountain range

**instrument** machine that helps you do something

**lava** hot, melted rock that erupts from a volcano

**metal** hard, shiny material

**mine** hole dug in the ground to get something valuable, such as metals or coal

**mountaineer** someone who climbs mountains

**national park** large area of countryside that is protected so people can enjoy its beauty

**range** several mountains grouped together

**satellite** object put into space that can take photographs or send TV signals, for example

**sea level** height of the surface of the sea

**ski lift** something that carries skiers up a hill or mountain

**summit** top of a mountain

**terrace** flat area of land dug into the side of a mountain

**volcano** place where lava escapes through a hole in the ground

# More Books to Read

Ashwell, Miranda, and Andy Owen. *Mountains.* Chicago: Heinemann Library, 1998.

Fowler, Allan. *Living in the Mountains.* Danbury, Conn.: Scholastic Library, 2000.

Gaff, Jackie. *I Wonder Why Mountains Have Snow on Top: And Other Questions about Mountains.* Boston: Houghton Mifflin, 2004.

Galko, Francine. *Mountain Animals.* Chicago: Heinemann Library, 2003.

Geisert, Bonnie, and Arthur Geisert. *Mountain Town.* Boston: Houghton Mifflin, 2000.

Kramer, Sydelle A. *To the Top!: Climbing the World's Highest Mountain.* New York: Random House Children's Books, 2004.

Llewellyn, Claire. *Volcanoes.* Chicago: Heinemann Library, 2000.

# Index